DIARY OF THE
CAT NAMED
Carrot

Erin Merryn

Health Communications, Inc.
Boca Raton, Florida

www.hcibooks.com

**Library of Congress Cataloging-in-Publication Data
is available through the Library of Congress**

© 2021 Erin Merryn

ISBN-13: 978-07573-2390-4 (Hardcover)
ISBN-10: 07573-2390-1 (Hardcover)
ISBN-13: 978-07573-2391-1 (ePub)
ISBN-10: 07573-2391-X (ePub)

HCI, its Logos and Marks are trademarks of Health Communications, Inc.

Publisher: Health Communications, Inc.
        1700 NW 2nd Avenue
        Boca Raton, FL 33432-1653

Cover design by Larissa Hise Henoch
Interior design and formatting by Lawna Patterson Oldfield

A Note from Erin

Many of you know the story of my cat Bailey, the subject of my book *Bailey, No Ordinary Cat,* and whose image went viral after I posted video of my daughter Abby singing "You Are My Sunshine" to him. Bailey was a very special cat with a gentle nature who sadly died shortly before the book was published. After his passing, I had no plans of getting another cat. There was no way we'd find another Bailey—or even one that would come close to having a personality like his. Mainly, I didn't want to disappoint my girls and possibly end up with a cat that was defensive and fearful of humans. I had cats like this growing up, but it is different when your first cat is so remarkable like theirs was.

As time passed, the thought of getting another cat kept coming into my head. It's good for children to grow up with pets. It teaches them kindness and responsibility. *Was I wrong about not getting another cat? Should I reconsider my decision?* I prayed for an answer, believing that God would lead me in the right direction as He had in the past.

As luck would have it, a woman named Jennifer, who had followed Bailey on social media, was fostering a pregnant mama cat, an orange tabby like Bailey. She reached out to me a few

Bailey, in costume, relaxing in the doll cradle.

months after he died and then wrote, "The kittens were born, and when they are a little older the girls can come meet them if you would like." As you will read a few pages into this book, one of those kitties was Carrot (though at first they thought she was a boy, and named her Noah). It was too coincidental; I felt

Carrot, lounging in the same cradle.

it was a sign that Bailey led us to her. It was love at first sight, and we soon welcomed Carrot into our family. Her personality blossomed, and we discovered that she was just as special as Bailey—sweet, gentle, and always willing to let the girls dress her in costumes and take her for rides in their toy car.

Some people think Carrot is Bailey reincarnated because they are so similar. While Bailey and Carrot have a lot of similarities, they definitely have their differences. Bailey was terrified of the vacuum cleaner and of plastic bags. Carrot loves to attack plastic bags and follows me into each room while I vacuum. Like most cats, Bailey would not budge if you put a leash on him. Carrot will walk on a leash like a dog. Carrot likes to snuggle, but she also enjoys her space. Bailey never wanted to stop snuggling, and I loved that about him—though I sometimes couldn't get anything done because he always wanted to be in my lap!

Bailey was a senior cat when my girls were born, but with Carrot they get to experience a kitten. The neat thing is, they are all growing up together. The book that follows is a journey through our first year together—from Carrot's point of view!

Both Bailey and Carrot have enriched our lives immeasurably, and I can truly say they are a part of our family. I know that my girls will never forget either of them. So many cats—and dogs—are living in shelters across the country. I hope this book might inspire you to open your heart and home to an animal in need.

Erin Merryn

I came into this world in the afternoon on April Fool's Day and started my life with a big surprise. My human foster mom named me "Noah" but I was actually a girl! It was an honest mistake because 80 percent of ginger cats like me are boys. I have four siblings: three brothers named Walter, Winston, and Ethan and one sister, Stevie. My mama's name is Peach, but I never met my dad. Mama was pregnant when she was dropped off at the shelter and she never saw Dad again. I can tell she misses him. There are some other cats that live here, but Mama hisses at them if they get too close to us. She is very protective.

My littermates and I had visitors today:
two little girls, their mom, and a baby. "Be nice!
No scratching!" Mama purred. The oldest girl, Abby,
held me a lot. The mom told the other girl, Hannah,
to be gentle with us. She hasn't seen how rough
we play! They talked about missing their cat Bailey,
who died, so now they go to shelters and play with
cats that have no homes. When it was time for the
girls to leave, Abby begged her mom to take one of
us home, but she said, "No, your dad won't allow
it." "We don't have to tell him. We'll hide the kitten
in our room." Abby said. The mom and our human
Jennifer laughed, then Jennifer said that we were
still too little to leave our mom. Phew! I was getting
nervous. They hugged us goodbye. Abby and Hannah
looked sad that they were leaving.

JUNE 3

Mama gathered us all together on our bed this morning for a talk. Her whiskers twitched, which meant it was serious. Ethan probably peed on the carpet again and is going to blame one of us, or maybe Stevie pooped over the side of the litter box as usual. It turned out we weren't in trouble—but something worse. Mama told us we were going to the shelter tomorrow where we would be for a few days and then find our separate forever homes. We curled up around Mama and cried. I asked her, "What if I don't like my forever home?" She promised me I would go to a place filled with love and happiness, that I needed to trust her.

I hope she is right.

JUNE 4

Jennifer took us to the shelter today. We were scared, but the nice people there put us all together in a cage at the front door by a window. We sat with Mama on a big cat tree. As I looked outside, I saw familiar faces—the mom and girls who visited us! Did they know we were here? A shelter worker took me and two of my siblings to a room where the mom and the girls played with us for a while but then left. Maybe they just came here on their weekly cat visit, or maybe they wanted to see us again before we got adopted. I just hope I go to a home with a sweet family with little kids like these girls. They are a lot of fun.

At last, I found my "furver" home—not just anyone, but the family with the three girls! My new mom placed me in a gated area of a room. Claire, the baby, saw me and got really excited. No sign of Abby or Hannah, then Mom said I was going to be a birthday surprise for them since they were born six days apart. Soon they came running down the stairs to a table of gifts that they ripped open excitedly. Then Hannah stopped and squealed, "There is a kitty!" Abby saw me next and fell to the ground shouting, "Mommy, thank you, thank you, thank you!" They took turns holding me, then Claire crawled into the room and Mom got as excited as the girls. She said, "I've been trying to get you to crawl for a month!" I guess I was the secret sauce! Mom said, "What should we name her?" Immediately, Abby said, "Carrot!"

The sun was just poking up over the horizon today when Abby and Hannah raced downstairs to see me. Before long, they were fighting over who got to hold me. Mom sat them down and talked to them about taking turns. They have all sorts of fun toys that I didn't have at my foster home, like a doll stroller. They pushed me around all over the house in it and I liked it so much they took me outside, too. I also got to try new food today. I'm not sure what it was, but it was yummy. The best part is that the girls put me in a chair and fed me with a teeny spoon. The baby, Claire, sure does get excited to see me. She tries to crawl after me, but I am faster than she is.

JUNE 26

Day 3 and I'm really settling in! Baby Claire seems to get up before her sisters, so we have a lot of alone time. Mom stayed right by her side, maybe so she didn't hurt me. Mom took her by the hand and showed her how to gently stroke my back. She gets so excited she tries to squeeze me. Mom keeps saying, "Claire, I've never seen you this happy!" She might be right, every time I see her, she's smiling. She likes when Mom puts me in the high chair next to her while she eats. I like to lick her fingers to get a taste of what she is having. Mmmm, sweet potatoes and bananas are my favorites!

The girls read me a bunch of books today. Actually, they aren't reading the words but they make up a story by looking at the pictures on each page. One of the books they read was called, *Bailey, No Ordinary Cat*. It is about their cat that crossed the Rainbow Bridge six months ago.

The book is filled with pictures of him. They dressed him up in all kinds of human clothes and even took baths with him! I can tell they miss him by the sad look they get in their eyes when they talk about him. I hope they end up loving me as much as they loved him. I have some big paws to fill!

I have been in my new home for a week. There is so much love and happiness here. Every day is a new adventure with these girls. Today they gave me a "peticure." The girls just pretended to use nail polish. Mom said she wouldn't let them use the real thing because that's dangerous. After that, she put these caps over my claws that were sparkly gold! She knows kitties want to stretch their claws on stuff, like the furniture, and this is a way to keep us both happy. I got used to the caps pretty quickly, and I think I look real fancy now. After the girls saw how cool my claws looked they asked Mom to paint their nails.

I haven't mentioned it before, but there is actually one guy in this house: my new human dad. He doesn't pay much attention to me during the day, and at first I didn't think he liked me, but at night, when the house is quiet after the girls are asleep, he likes to play with me. He gets out my toys and has me chasing them. We play a game where he moves his hand toward me like a creeping animal. I lunge forward to attack it. Another favorite thing is when he turns on the laser light. I chase it all over the house. It's fun but exhausting! Even though I am a kitten, I am totally pooped after these play sessions. Dad's a little camera-shy, but he's pretty cool guy, and I can tell he really loves his family.

JULY 4

We took a very long car ride today—the humans call it a "road trip." At first I cried a lot because I was stuck in a cage. I tired myself out and fell asleep. When I woke up, we were at our destination: a lake house owned by my mom's parents. We went on a fun ride—not nearly as long—on a golf cart in a parade to celebrate America's birthday. I didn't see presents or cake but it was fun. Later, we all went down by the lake. Bailey might have liked water— I saw pictures of him in a bathtub—but I don't, so I stayed on dry land. Right next to the water was the biggest litter box I have ever seen. I was shocked when I saw all these little kids playing in it! They poured buckets of litter all over themselves. Yuk! Don't they know what you are supposed to do here? It is nighttime now, but I can't sleep. There are these loud booms coming from the sky that are scaring me. I purr to calm myself down.

JULY 8

We had so much fun on the road trip that today we pretended to go on another one, just me and the girls. Hannah put me in a car seat. Abby was the driver. Claire and I sat next to each other in back. Claire tried strapping me in, but it was not comfortable. Abby helped me but, wow, Claire can get really loud! Every time I started to take a catnap, she'd start screaming—not mad, just excited. Dogs do that, too. These girls play so nicely together; they don't tumble around and nip at each other like my brothers, sister, and I used to. I miss them, but I'm happy here.

I sleep a lot, just like Claire. I've heard that babies and kittens need a lot of sleep because we are growing. I fall asleep a lot in the girls' laps. Every night at bedtime the girls ask if I can sleep with them, but Mom won't allow it. She tells them that when I get bigger I can. Mom lets me fall asleep in her bed in the evening and then brings me downstairs to my bed when she and Dad go to sleep. All this talk of sleep is making me drowsy . . .

AUGUST 6

My human mom's name is Erin. She grew up with several cats, unlike Dad. She actually adopted me before even telling Dad. She let him know about me in a Father's Day card, telling him he was going to be a dad to another girl—just one with fur, four legs, and a tail! He was okay with it because he knew how much joy Bailey brought to them. Mom is a pretty busy lady. She is a full-time mom, author, and activist. When she isn't busy taking care of us girls, she is working on passing a law across America called Erin's Law, designed to protect kids from abuse. It is close to passing in all 50 states!

AUGUST 17

The girls pampered me like a queen today.
They put me in a chair and gave me a massage.
I even got to drink water out of a glass! It was a little
strange at first, but then I liked it better than the
big bowl I usually use. At lunchtime, Abby and
Hannah had turkey sandwiches. Don't tell Mom,
but they sneak me turkey, which makes me so
excited I climb on the table hoping to get more of
their food. *Hmm,* maybe that's why Mom puts me
in the basement when they eat!

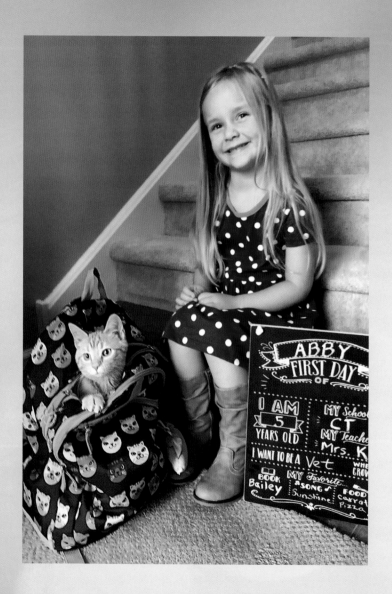

AUGUST 19

This was a big day in our household: Abby's first day of kindergarten. Mom took pictures of her with a sign so she'd always remember it. While they were busy doing that, I jumped into Abby's backpack. Maybe I could go to school with her without Mom knowing! Just when I thought I was free and clear, she said, "Nice try, Carrot, but you can't go with her!" Darn! Abby was really excited to take the school bus with all the other big kids. They all went outside and waited at the end of the driveway for the bus while I watched from the window. As the bus rolled up, Mom gave Abby kisses goodbye. When Mom came back inside, she was crying. I know how she feels. I'll miss Abby, too!

AUGUST 26

Abby wasn't the only one starting school. Today was Hannah's first day of preschool. I tried to sneak in her backpack, too, but Mom caught me again. Moms really *must* have eyes in the backs of their heads. "No kittens allowed at Hannah's school. You get to stay home with Claire," she said. I watched from the window while Mom drove off with Hannah. I took a nap to kill time, but woke to a smack on the head. Ouch! I looked up to see Claire laughing. She doesn't understand how to be gentle. She likes to crawl after me, but I am faster on all fours than she is. Mom just put her down for her nap, so I am going to go finish mine.

AUGUST 27

We played dress-up today. The girls put me in tutus and bows. They even put Mom's pearls on me, but I don't think they asked her if it was okay because when Mom saw what I was wearing she was *not* happy. She had a talk with them about not taking her things without asking. She told them the pearls were not a toy and to put their own princess necklaces on me. Even though Mom wasn't pleased about the necklace, she did say it looked very pretty on me!

SEPTEMBER 1

I'm five months old today. Mama dressed me up and took pictures. She likes to put me in tutus, too. She does the same with Claire. Claire is six months older than me. The girls dressed up Bailey a lot in girl outfits but he was a boy. They say I am so much like Bailey. Abby says that I *am* Bailey and came back as a girl because he didn't like all the dresses he had to wear when he was a boy. What they don't know is that my first night with them, Mom had a long talk with me about Bailey. From the things she said, I think we would have liked each other. I hope I make them as happy as he did.

SEPTEMBER 8

The weather was nice, so we played outside today. The girls have a pink kid-sized car they drive on the sidewalk. Abby is the only one who knows how to drive it. When Hannah takes a turn she usually ends up in the grass and Mom has to come pull us out. I either sit on Hannah's lap or Claire's. They have me on a leash, but I won't run away. I might take off chasing a bird, but I know where home is. I would come back.

SEPTEMBER 13

I like being dressed up. Most cats would hate it but, honestly, I like the attention. Mom tells me everyone is unique in their own way. Some cats prefer peace and quiet; this would definitely not be the home for them! I have so much fun playing with my human sisters. Baby Claire does need to be supervised, though. She sure can get a tight grip on me. She also likes to play with my whiskers, which doesn't really bother me. I'm sure any other cat would scratch or bite her. I know she doesn't mean any harm; she's just enthusiastic.

OCTOBER 2

Claire's birthday was today, and she had a cat-themed party! She even wore an outfit that said her name on it with a picture of a ginger cat. It was all so exciting that I started playing with the decorations and made them fall down. Mom wasn't happy with me. She warned me to stop or she'd have to put me in the basement the rest of the day. Soon, people started showing up and the house filled up with kids fast. They all wanted to hold me, and I kept hearing the adults telling them to take turns with me. One little girl seemed like she had never held a cat before and tried walking away with me! They had pizza for dinner, but not me. I have the same boring food every day. I was hoping someone would sneak some pepperoni to me. After dinner, everyone sang to Claire and she ate her birthday cake. Yum! Don't tell her this, but I think I got more attention from all the kids than she did.

OCTOBER 8

Mom blew up a bunch of balloons for the girls to play with. They passed them back and forth, and I decided to join the fun. I would try to beat them to the balloon as they threw it in the air. The girls might be bigger than me, but I can jump really high. Did you know that cats can jump six times their body length? Mom recorded us playing. She kept warning me that my nails could pop the balloon and it would make a loud noise and scare me. I didn't care, I was having too much fun. I was pretty tired after that, so guess what? I took a long nap.

Today we played school. Abby is almost always the teacher when we play. She used an easel that I climbed up on. Claire doesn't have the patience for playing school. She always gets distracted. Abby starts us with the "word of the day." Today's word was "cat." I approve! Abby is learning how to read and wants to show us how she does it. The girls were having so much fun that when it was time for bed they didn't want to stop. Begging Mom to stay up rarely works—especially on a school night.

Abby is married. Well, not really—she's just a kid, after all—but she has this imaginary husband named Brad. She is always talking to him on her toy phone. Sometimes, I think she really is talking to someone. She could be an actress. Poor Brad is always in some kind of trouble with her. Sometimes, though, she tells him she wants more cats. Maybe Brad will get her some imaginary cats, but she won't get any more real ones from Mom and Dad. This is fine with me. I don't need another cat to have fun. I have all the fun in the world with these three girls.

OCTOBER 18

I play all sorts of fun games with the girls.
They have so many toys for me to play with, I think
I might have more toys than they do. Dad might
disagree about that. He thinks they have too many
toys. He has a system, though, that if new toys come
in, old toys need to go out. He tells the girls those
toys will go to kids who are less fortunate than they
are. That makes everyone happy.

Tonight, we carved pumpkins. Hannah carved a face and Abby did a kitty cat. They turned out great, but it was really messy. There are all these seeds and wet, stringy things in the pumpkins that you have to pull out. Mom is so smart! She washed the seeds and cooked them in the oven. When they were done cooking, the girls got to eat them.

I licked a few of them and, man, did they taste good! Mom said it's the salt she added to them. After we finished, she put candles in the pumpkins, and then she took them to the front porch and lit them. They looked so cool!

The girls love to bake with Mom—especially cookies. Today, we baked her favorite: peanut butter. Abby and Hannah took turns putting ingredients in a big bowl. Mom pushed a button, and, like magic, this machine mixed everything together. We rolled the dough into balls and mashed them down with a fork. Mom put the cookies in the oven and turned on the light so we could watch them bake. Mmm mmm, they smelled good! When they were done, each girl got one. Hannah wanted to share with me, but Mom said, "Carrot will get sick eating that. She has to stick to cat food." Doesn't she know I'm tired of cat food? Hannah must know, because she snuck me a piece when Mom wasn't looking.

Today is Halloween and guess what? It snowed! I've never seen this stuff before. Everyone was saying it was too early for snow, even here in Illinois. Mom knew this was a big deal for me, so she took me outside. Wow, I thought it was going to be soft and warm, like cotton, but it was kind of hard and cold on my paws! The girls dressed up to go trick-or-treating. Abby was a crazy cat lady. What's so crazy about that? Hannah was a veterinarian. Please, just don't give me any shots! Claire was a domino. She is obsessed with these things and carries one around almost all the time. Then there was my costume. Since my name is Carrot, Mom thought it would be fun to dress me up as one. I didn't get to go out with the girls, which was fine with me. I stayed home with Dad and helped him hand out candy.

NOVEMBER 1

Look what came in the mail today! Matching pajamas for the girls, and they had carrots all over them! Wow, was this all for me? After we put them on, Mom gathered us all on the couch to take a photo, and then the girls and I ran around the house. I would hide in a corner and jump out as they ran by. Claire isn't walking yet, but she is getting close. She tries to catch me, but I am too fast.

NOVEMBER 3

I hardly walked today. First, Claire pushed me in a kid-sized shopping cart. I think it is helping her learn how to walk. Then Abby pushed me around in this toy motor home of Hannah's. I just sat there while they pushed me all over the house in it. Later in the day, Hannah put me in her doll stroller and covered me with blankets. She has actual baby dolls, but I think she likes me better. Claire gets mad when she has to share me with her sisters. Mom explains to the girls she is only one year old and doesn't understand having to share yet.

NOVEMBER 8

Mom and the girls went to the mall today.
They came home with all kinds of goodies for me:
funny looking glasses that were way too big and a
bunch of new bows for my head. I was surprised
when they woke me up to try these things on.
I am one spoiled kitty. I think they buy more stuff
for me than for themselves.

News alert! Claire is walking. I'm pretty sure
it is because of me. I did teach her how to crawl,
remember? So how did this happen? Mom put
Claire on one side of the family room and told her
to walk across the room to Hannah. No go. She
just wanted to sit on Mom's lap. Then Mom put me
on the other side of the room in the stroller. She
held Claire's hands as she stood on the carpet and
said, "Go walk to kitty." She said it over and over.
The first few times Claire was too excited and kept
falling down. On the fourth try, she walked right to
me. Mom jumped up and down, she was so excited.
"Good job, Claire, you walked to kitty! Do it again!"
And she did, many times. I wondered how humans
did this. Now I know. Do they all have cats to train
them?

Besides catnapping and playing with the
girls, one of my favorite activities is snuggling.
Since I can't talk like a human can, it's my way of
saying, "I love you." I got in a lot of snuggle time
with Hannah today. She gets me all to herself
when Abby goes to school and Claire takes a nap.
I usually sit next to her while she plays in her
dollhouse. She talks to me like a human and sings
me sweet songs. It doesn't last long enough.
Before we know it, Claire is up and ready to lay
on me or squeeze me. Ooof, she's getting bigger
by the day!

NOVEMBER 16

I'm teaching Claire all kinds of new things, but Mom isn't necessarily happy about all of them. Claire does not crawl anymore and is getting faster on her two feet. I went upstairs and she followed me. I was as surprised as anyone, because Mom had only turned her back for thirty seconds and Claire was right behind me, giggling the whole way. Mom came running and grabbed her, then explained that she could get hurt. I don't think she was paying attention, because she tried it again later. Mom put me in the basement so she could get some things done without worrying about Claire. I really didn't mind; at least in the basement I can get some sleep.

NOVEMBER 27

We are celebrating again. This time, it's something called Thanksgiving. Mom said it is a day to celebrate the people we are thankful for in our lives. For me, that is this wonderful family that adopted me. I miss my mom and littermates, but I have been blessed with a new family filled with love. The best part of today was that the whole house smelled like turkey—my favorite! Abby put a plate of food in front of me saying it was my Thanksgiving dinner, but then I realized it was toy food, all plastic! Luckily, Mom gave me some real turkey. After dinner, everyone ate pumpkin pie. I wonder if this is from Halloween? Mom said I couldn't have any because I would get sick. When she wasn't looking, Hannah let me lick a little off her finger so I could at least get a taste. If only someone could create a pie like this for cats, I'd be in heaven.

DECEMBER 1

Mom bought me a new present—a tree, and it is HUGE! Wow, I didn't know you could bring a tree in the house. It kind of looks like a pine tree, but it sure doesn't smell like one. Mom asked everyone to spread the branches out. Abby and Hannah did a good job, but Claire didn't quite get the hang of it. Then Mom hit a button and the whole tree lit up like magic! They put a bunch of sparkly objects on the tree that they called "ornaments." Half of them seem to be ginger cats. It's really nice of them to decorate my tree like this. We finished, then put funny hats on and Mom took our picture in front of our masterpiece. I can't wait to climb this thing!

DECEMBER 3

I have discovered the tree isn't for me after all. It is for another holiday—Christmas. I don't quite understand it, but you set a tree up and somebody named "Santa Claus" flies around the world and brings presents on the night before Christmas—Christmas Eve—but, not for adults, only kids, and only *good* boys and girls. Mom has told the girls they have to stay on the "nice list" or they won't get any presents. Wow, harsh! I think I am on the "naughty list," because I keep climbing in the tree and Mom gets angry. I just can't help it. This thing is fun. I've tried hiding in the branches, but she keeps finding me, or the girls will tell her where I am. I wish I was green instead of orange. Mom tells me I will break the branches and ruin the tree. Sorry, Mom, but this is better than any toy I have *ever* had.

DECEMBER 5

Tonight, Mom had the girls sit at the table and write letters to this guy Santa to tell him what they want when he makes his big trip around the world in one night. It must be an extremely big sleigh. Abby wrote that she really wanted a camera. I have no idea what Claire wants. Then Hannah asked Santa for a big cardboard box. I love boxes—like all cats—but I didn't know kids did, too. I'm hoping she gets it so I can play in it. Does Santa bring gifts to animals? I hope so. If he does, I would like to request a cat tree so I have another place to curl up and take naps. And catnip. You can never have enough catnip!

DECEMBER 7

We did a really fun project today with Mom.
We made ornaments for the Christmas tree. The
girls helped her mix this powder and water together,
then Mom poured it in front of them on a plate.
The girls put their hands into this gloppy stuff to
make their handprint. Then it was my turn, and
I placed my paw into it. Cool! After they were dry,
Mom wrote our names and the year on the back.
Once they were done, we got to put them on the
Christmas tree.

DECEMBER 10

Mom said she is going to take the Christmas tree down if she catches me climbing in it one more time. Oh, man, I don't want to ruin it for everyone! I've already broken two branches, and Mom is really annoyed about it. She got out the baby gate and put it across the tree to stop me, but she wasn't thinking too clearly when she came up with this idea. I just climbed up that gate and back into the tree. I hid and tried to stay stock-still, but she saw me anyway. I tried to climb to the top before she could grab me, but I wasn't fast enough. She put me in the basement and didn't let me back out until it was time for dinner.

DECEMBER 15

This morning, Mom told the girls that if they are good all day and get along, she would have a treat at the end of the day for them. They listened, and after dinner she made them hot cocoa. She topped it with marshmallows and whipped cream. Abby asked if I could have some, too, but Mom said it would make me sick. She filled my cup with water instead. Mom does let me have whipped cream sometimes—but just a little bit. Some mornings, she squirts a little bit in each of our mouths. It is my absolute favorite treat. I beg for it every time she opens the refrigerator.

After we watched Abby get on the bus and go to real school, we played school. Hannah was the teacher and Claire and I were the students.

I am the teacher's pet—for real! I sit down and pay attention to Miss Hannah, but Claire gets easily distracted. Hannah is only teacher when Abby is not home. Hannah teaches us things she is learning in preschool. Every day, they go over the weather outside. Today it is cold and rainy. I always wonder where all the stray cats go in the bad weather. She has also been learning how to count. She is trying to teach Claire to say she is "one." It is really fun to watch big sister teach her little sister.

DECEMBER 24

It is finally Christmas Eve. Santa is coming tonight, and I get to find out if he leaves presents for kitty cats. After a family Christmas party, Mom, Dad, and the girls came home to put cookies and milk out for Santa. I'm sure he gets hungry after all that traveling and gift-giving. The girls were all excited to leave the cookies for Santa and they also gave him a carrot. Wow, does he really like vegetables? Maybe yes, maybe no, but apparently his reindeer *love* carrots. After everyone went to bed, I jumped up on the table and drank some of the milk. Well, okay, I drank almost all of it. They will *never* know it was me!

DECEMBER 25

Mom and Dad got up early and put on Christmas music. The girls ran downstairs to the Christmas tree to find a pile of presents. Hannah's jaw dropped when she saw the *huge* box in the corner of the room for her. How did Santa fit that thing in his sleigh? It was filled with balloons. Hannah and I immediately climbed inside it to play. We were having so much fun that Hannah didn't want to stop and open the rest of her presents. Abby got the camera she had asked for. I think she took at least a hundred pictures before the day was over. Many of them were of me. And guess what? I got a present after all! I got my new cat tree, where I took a long nap this morning after we opened presents. Claire got some toys but she was most interested in that big box. We played in it all day.

DECEMBER 31

Claire and I fell asleep together on the floor today. Mom said we are both growing and need our rest. Claire chased me all over the house. We were both tired after that. Tomorrow starts a new year. The past year of my life has been an adventure and a half: from my short time spent with my mom and siblings, to the very brief time in the shelter, then finding my forever home. I wonder what the next year will bring?

JANUARY 3

I woke up from my nap to see Mom and the girls taking all the ornaments off the tree. She said Christmas is over and it is time for the tree to come down. Wow, that was quick! I felt like we just put the tree up. I tried my best to stop her from putting it away. I climbed in the branches and refused to get out even as she tried to put everything in the big storage bins. Eventually, everything was cleaned up and put away until next Christmas. Luckily for me, I still have this huge box to play with. Hannah likes to hide in there with me away from her sisters. She snuggles with me inside the box with blankets.

JANUARY 9

Guess what happened today? I got married. No, not really. It was all pretend with the girls. Abby put me in a wedding dress and Hannah put one of their stuffed animal cats in a suit. They called my groom "Bob." I'm not sure where that name came from. Abby held a Bible and pretended to read from it. Claire wanted nothing to do with this wedding ceremony and kept trying to interrupt it. She took my veil and tried to run away with it. She also kept grabbing Bob and attempted to throw him in the garbage. Abby and Hannah laughed. Abby thought Claire was jealous and didn't want me to marry Bob. Finally, Abby had enough of Claire interrupting the wedding ceremony and asked Mom to come get her. Claire was not happy and sat herself down right next to me and wouldn't budge. She held me tight and Mom said, "Well it looks like Claire is objecting to this marriage." And then everyone started laughing.

I am a mommy now—to pretend kittens.
They came with a stuffed animal the girls got for
Christmas. The girls are now placing the kittens
around me and saying I am the mommy and they
have their baby dolls. I will never be able to be a
real mommy with kittens since I got spayed at the
shelter. I think it would be fun to have my own
babies, but I understand why humans spay us.
There are so many cats in shelters with no homes.
Stray cats are having babies all the time and many
of them live on the street. By spaying and neutering
cats, it helps control the population of cats so that
shelters are not overwhelmed—but many are already.
I know that I was one of the lucky ones.

JANUARY 19

It is not a fun day in our home. Abby and Hannah are both sick and have been on the couch all day. The girls were so sick that Mom and Dad were up all night crying, and Mom took them to the doctor this morning. I don't like seeing them this way. They seem sad, and they don't want to eat or play; they just want to watch television or sleep. I wish I could make them better, but I don't know how to do that. I snuggle up with them on the couch. I put them to sleep to the sound of my purr.

JANUARY 22

I'm not sure who invented this thing called a "donut," but it is pretty awesome. When Mom was in the office looking for something, I pushed the pantry door open. Claire saw me do it and grabbed a bag of donuts that were in a basket low enough for her to reach. She hid in a corner of the house and I followed her. I knew these treats were special because Claire started shoving them in her mouth and giggling, and then she let me lick the sweet powdered sugar off them. Our fun didn't last long. We looked up and there was Mom, standing over us, looking none too happy. We had been caught red-pawed. Mom took the bag of donuts from Claire. She was sure Abby and Hannah had left the pantry door open. I just strolled away like nothing had happened.

JANUARY 24

I got a day at the spa today. Abby and Hannah put me in a pink robe, gave me a facial, and pretended to paint my claws. Do other cats have a glam squad like I do? I sure do love all this attention. Claire was napping. If she were around, she would not want them doing this to me. She wants me all to herself. Mom is constantly trying to teach her how to share and take turns.

JANUARY 25

Today I went to the doctor. Not a real veterinarian but "Dr. Abby." First, she listened to my heart. Then she looked inside my mouth, nose, and ears. "What clean ears she has!" she told Mom. Then she gave me shots, but they didn't hurt since it was all pretend. She gave me a healthy report. Mom has talked about taking me to the real vet when I turn one in April. I thought you only go to the doctor if you are sick! I am really scared to go. I still remember going to the doctor when I was a little kitten and got real shots. It hurt! I hope I don't need those again.

Every day, Mom puts a dish of fresh water down for me. But I never drink from it. I like to drink directly from a glass cup like all the humans; it's fresher than the stuff that has been sitting out all day. Mom doesn't know it, but when she is not looking I drink out of her glass or Dad's glass of water. I also like drinking out of the toilet, as I've heard dogs like to do. Mom really hates it when she catches me doing this! I try to be sneaky, but I always seem to get caught in the act. She is constantly telling the girls to keep the bathroom door closed so I cannot get in there. They almost always forget.

FEBRUARY 3

I got to enjoy the great outdoors today.
I love being outside. There was snow on the ground,
so Mom dressed me in this really cute pink coat
and hat to keep me warm. I prefer warmer weather,
but walking on the snow doesn't bother me that
much and it was sunny. It's also nice to just sit
by the front door and enjoy some fresh air.
I can't wait until spring.

Mom has started a routine of having Abby read me books at night. Since Abby is just learning, Mom will read the book to her first and see how she does at reading it back to me. It's so relaxing, sometimes I fall asleep. Then I am woken up to Hannah picking me up and bringing me to her bed saying it is her turn to read to me. She is only three, so she cannot read but she does a great job making up the story from the pictures in the book. I usually like their choices—they have a lot of books about cats!

It is Valentine's Day: a day all about love.
I smelled something really nice and followed my
nose to the kitchen where I found beautiful flowers
Dad bought for Mom. He also gave her chocolate.
When the girls saw that, they asked for some before
they even had breakfast. Mom dressed all of us up
in red, pink, and white. I got to wear a red tutu—
good thing I'm a girl! Mom surprised the girls later
with their own heart-shaped box of chocolate.
She told them how much she loved them, but
she tells them that every day!

FEBRUARY 16

I was named for an orange vegetable, Carrot,
but if I had been green my name could have been
Cucumber instead. I had never seen one before
and Mom put it on the ground to see if it was true
what they say about cats being totally flummoxed by
these things. But I'm not like most cats, and I wasn't
confused or scared at all. After slowly investigating,
I had all sorts of fun rolling it all over the kitchen
floor. Mom couldn't stop laughing, and the best part
was when she went to take it back and I wouldn't let
her have it. I bit it over and over again with my sharp
teeth so she gave up and let me keep it.

It was a rainy day so we could not go outside and play. The girls wanted to do another spa day with me—they really love these things—but this time they went all out. After putting me in a cute robe and cleaning my paws, Hannah started me out with a pawicure. Abby pretended to wash my face and then placed cucumber slices on my eyes. I'm not kidding! I have no idea why humans put part of their salad on their eyelids but I let them do it. Mom put on relaxing spa music, then Abby and Hannah lay down next to me and also got the cucumber treatment while we listened to ocean sounds. It was so relaxing that—guess what?—I fell asleep.

FEBRUARY 26

I got a very big surprise today! This morning, a woman came over with a cat. I have not been around other cats since I left the shelter. I was not happy, and when she approached me I hissed over and over again. Her name was Bing and she walked all over the house, smelling every room. She acted like she owned the place. I followed her, keeping my distance. She completely ignored me, but then she started eating my food, which really made me mad. As I got closer to her, a familiar scent hit me. She smelled just like my mama did. I don't remember what she looked like—I left her when I was so young—but I could never forget her smell. "Mama is that you?" I climbed up on a chair trying to get another look at her face. She smiled at me. "Yes, I have a new name. I promised you your forever family would be wonderful. I see that I was right." She told me she loved me and I told her I loved her back. As much as I miss her, I would never want to leave my home.

After we watched Abby get on the school bus,
Mom pulled out paper and markers for us to draw.
She put Claire down for a nap because she is too
little to play with markers. If she sees us with them
she starts to get really upset if we don't give her
any. Claire has gotten into the markers before
after Abby and Hannah forgot to put them away,
and she drew all over the wall. When Mom saw the
mess on the walls and asked who did it. Abby
and Hannah both said, "Claire," but Claire said,
"Kitty," blaming me for being naughty. Maybe it's
just because she doesn't know how to say "Abby"
or "Hannah." We ended up drawing pictures of
ourselves. I think mine turned out pretty close to
what I actually look like!

MARCH 9

When Abby gets home from school, Mom gives us all a snack. Today, she decided on carrots. Abby loves carrots with ranch dressing. I have never eaten carrots before, but she thought I should give them a try. *Blecch!* Now I see why Hannah doesn't like them. They are nasty! When I wouldn't eat them, Mom poured some of my own tuna juice over them to see if that would make them taste better for me. I licked up all the juice but didn't touch the carrots. When Mom wasn't looking, Hannah put a bunch of her carrots on my plate so that it looked like she ate hers. Mom caught her, so that was the end of that!

MARCH 10

Now that it is starting to get warmer, Mom is going outside with us more and more. I noticed that you really start to hear the birds outside. I watch them from the window. I wish I could freely roam the outside. Mom shared a story with the girls about Bailey. He used to be a free-range cat, but one day he didn't come home. He was gone for a week. Mom found him trapped under someone's house. There are lots of coyotes outside that would love to have me for dinner. I am allowed to go outside if Mom is outside with me or if I am on a leash. Everything in me wants to take off after the birds, but Mom warns me that if I take off after a bird, I will lose my outdoor privileges altogether. Mom bought me a collar to wear. It has carrots all around it. That made me happy!

We did a lot today. I baked with Hannah while Abby was at school and Claire napped. When Abby came home, we played school. Normally, Hannah and Claire are the students with me. Today was different. It was a classroom of only cats. She called it the Ginger Academy. She made an entire classroom of ginger cats by taking all her stuffed animal cats and sitting them in front of her. She wears these silly pink glasses and dress-up shoes. She teaches us the sight words she is learning in kindergarten. I'll bet that she is going to grow up and be a teacher.

APRIL 1

Finally, it's my birthday! I was born exactly at 2:30 PM a year ago today. Mom had a fun party for me with the girls and all the ginger kitty stuffed animals. She decorated the room and got me a carrot cake—of course, what else? The cake was specially made by a bakery for cats and dogs so that it was safe for me. Mom got the girls their own carrot cake to eat. I didn't know what to wish for. I already had everything I ever wanted and that was a forever home. I got lots of new toys that the girls helped open. It was so fun. I can't wait until next year!

APRIL 9

I'm not the only one who had a birthday this month. Today is Dad's birthday and everyone was in a festive mood. We played dress-up and pretended we were going to a fancy ball. The girls put on dresses and sunglasses and they put me in a tutu and sunglasses, too. Then they danced to music in the family room. After dinner, we had cake and Mom pulled out last year's photo of Dad's birthday and got all teary-eyed. She couldn't believe how much we've all grown in a year—even me. I'm not a kitten anymore!

Besides two birthdays this month, we are celebrating Easter. I thought that only birds laid eggs, but there is a special rabbit called the Easter Bunny and he does as well. His eggs are many different colors and he hides them for children to find. He also leaves a basket on Easter morning full of candy and other cool stuff. We don't need to write to him to get this like we did with Santa Claus. In honor of this guy and of spring, we put on bunny ears and made fun, colorful cookies—flowers, bunnies, and, of course carrots!

Mom likes to take the girls on walks in forest preserves. On their walk today, they found a bunch of painted rocks along the path. Hannah found one with a paw print painted on it. Abby found one with a sun on it. She told Mom it was meant to be since "You Are My Sunshine" is her song that she sang to Bailey. Mom pulled out nail polish for the girls and me to paint our own rocks. Mom is always thinking of fun, creative ideas to do with us. I love it. Mom wrote positive uplifting words on the rocks. Tomorrow, the girls are going to go back out and place the rocks along the path for other people to find. We're spreading our own sunshine and happiness.

Mom took me outside this afternoon to enjoy the beautiful weather. I tried to run after two birds, but Abby had me on the leash. I tried a few more times and—wow—Abby accidentally dropped the leash. I came close, but I wasn't fast enough. Mom told me I needed to leave the birds alone, that those birds have babies they need to take care of and feed. She warned that if I did it again she would bring me inside. I instead decided to go after the chipmunk that dug a hole under the steps outside. It was really fast, and with Abby holding my leash there was no getting away to catch it. Tonight, we had a campfire outside. The girls helped Daddy make s'mores. Hannah had chocolate all over her face and very sticky hands. When Mom and Dad were not looking, she let me lick the remains of marshmallow off her fingers. I can always count on those girls for a sweet treat. They never leave me out!

Mom rewarded the girls for picking up all their toys and cleaning their rooms with movie night. She gave Abby and Hannah popcorn, Claire toddler puffs since she is too young for popcorn, and me a yummy cat treat covered in catnip. The movie was about horses because, after cats, they are their favorite animal. Abby and Hannah keep asking for a real horse for their birthdays, but Mom told them they would need a barn for an animal that big. Abby told Mom to go buy a barn, but she just laughed. She told them they would find someplace to go horseback riding instead. Claire has to sit right by me for the movie. It is funny that I was a birthday gift to Abby and Hannah, but Claire has pretty much taken me over and doesn't like sharing me. I'm sure the movie was good, but Claire and I fell asleep before it ended.

The girls and I had a big morning of fun playing house and crawling around on the floor pretending to be cats. Well, I didn't need to pretend! Then it was time for my nap. Mom bought me a new bed that hangs on the window. It's really comfortable and gives me the purr-fect view of the birds. The best part is that Claire can't reach it and wake me up—or so I thought. When Mom wasn't looking, she did a very cat-like move and got on top of my bed. She always needs to be near me. I wonder if she is part cat?

I've written about baking cookies with Mom and the girls. One of the ingredients is this white stuff called "flour." It sounds like the word "flower" but it does not smell like one. It kind of looks like snow, but it is not cold or wet. And it also kind of looks like sugar, but it is not sparkly, and it *definitely* does not taste good by itself! Mom took a work call this afternoon while Claire was having a snack in the kitchen, but she started getting loud, so Mom left the room. Claire wanted more and went looking in the pantry where she found the bag of flour. She forgot all about the snack and spilled the flour all over the floor. Before long, she was taking handfuls and throwing it in the air. We walked through it and made patterns with our hands and paws. It was loads of fun. I just hope we will have enough flour left to make cookies the next time Mom decides to bake something.

It was the last day of school for Abby today and she has come a long way since the first day. When she started kindergarten, she would make up the words in books when she read them to me. Now she can actually read some books. Mom pulled out the picture she took of Abby on the first day of kindergarten. It is amazing to see how much she has changed. Claire and Hannah have changed a lot, too. Claire wasn't walking or talking when Abby went off to her first day of school. Now she is running and saying a lot of words. Have I changed that much?

Mom was busy cleaning today while Claire took her nap. I thought I could help her when she was scrubbing the floors, so I jumped up to grab the mop leaning against the chair. Instead, I knocked it over and it fell to the floor. Oops! Mom laughed and said, "Carrot, that mop is too big for you. If you want to help, here is a sponge. Scrub the floors with that." She threw a sponge on the ground. Sure, I can do that! I ran to the sponge and dragged it across the floor. When Dad came home, he said the floors looked great! Mom told him I cleaned them.

JUNE 8

Mom's sister visited today with her sons—and her *huge* dog Duke! This is my first time meeting him. I hear he is a troublemaker who always gets into things. When he came into the house and saw me, he kept his distance. I decided to go sniff him out and he ran away. He kept trying to get away from me. Hah! Here he was this big dog and he is running away from a cat. Mom's sister kept trying to bring him close to me but he wasn't having it. Someone must have warned him about getting clawed by a cat. Then we went outside and once he saw I was on a leash he seemed to relax and got curious about me. He got kind of close and started to sniff me, so I bopped him on the nose with my paw—gently, of course—to let him know he was in my personal space. When he realized I wasn't going to hurt him, he lay down in the grass next to me until they left.

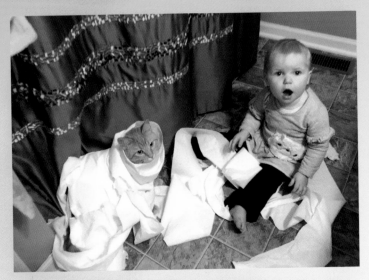

JUNE 15

I think Claire and I will be partners in crime for years to come. We are always getting into mischief together. Earlier today, Mom thought she had locked the gate to keep Claire from going anywhere. Well, she didn't have it latched all the way. Claire and I snuck upstairs and into the bathroom. She closed the door, grabbed the roll of toilet paper, and unrolled it all over the bathroom and then all over me. We were having so much fun we didn't hear Mom open the door. Claire said, "Uh oh!" She laughed and ran down the hall into her bedroom. Then she started pointing at me saying, "Kitty! Kitty!" Mom asked, "Did kitty make this mess?" Claire said, "Yes." I wasn't surprised. Claire always does. If only I could speak human. Still, I think Mom knows better!

JUNE 24

It's been a year since I was welcomed into my forever home. I feel like the luckiest cat in the world! I wish I could tell humans how important it is for anyone looking for a pet to adopt—not shop. Shelters are filled with animals waiting for their forever home. I only spent two days in one and it was scary. I don't think my family will adopt any more cats right now, and I am okay with that. I like being the only one. The girls and I have all grown up together. Baby Claire is now a busy toddler, and she is learning well how to be gentle with me, to talk, and to share me with Abby and Hannah, who are such great big sisters. I just have this feeling that there could be another crazy cat baby in this home again one day, and that will be a good thing. Any animal or child would be loved and blessed to be a part of this family.